T0023833

The Art of Prowling

by

Colonel G. A. Wade

With afterword by Philip Abbott

First published by Gale & Polden, c.1942

This edition published by Royal Armouries Museum,
Armouries Drive, Leeds LS10 1LT, United Kingdom
www.royalarmouries.org

Afterword by Philip Abbott © 2019 Trustees of the Royal Armouries
Parliamentary speech licensed under the Open Parliament Licence v3.0

ISBN 978 0 94809 292 3

A CIP record for this book is available from the British Library

Every effort has been made to contact copyright holders.
Royal Armouries will be happy to correct any errors or omissions
brought to their attention.

Typesetting by Typo•glyphix

Printed by Gomer Press

10 9 8 7 6 5 4 3 2 1

THE ART OF PROWLING

by

Colonel G. A. Wade

With afterword by Philip Abbott

THE HOME GUARD

The Prime Minister, Winston Churchill, to the House of Commons, 5 November 1940.

I turn to another of our dangers. Some of those very clever people who are sometimes wise after the event are now talking about "the invasion scare". I do not mind that, because it is true that the danger of invasion, particularly invasion by barges, has diminished with the coming of the winter months and the unpredictable uncertainty of the weather. It has also been diminished by the victories of the Royal Air Force and the ever-growing strength of the British Army. When I spoke at the end of June, I set forth in detail the well-known difficulties which would attend the invasion of these islands and which had been forgotten in years when we had not considered the matter at all. At that time, we had only a few brigades of well-armed and well-trained troops in this island. We had no Home Guard to deal with an invader or to deal with air-borne attacks behind the lines and the Royal Air Force had not then proved itself master of our own air by daylight.

Very different is the scene to-day. We have a very large Army here, improving in equipment and training continually. The main part of that Army is now highly mobile and is being constantly imbued with the spirit of counter-attack. We have 1,700,000 men in the Home Guard, all of whom will be in uniform by the end of this year and nearly all of whom are in uniform at this moment. Nearly 1,000,000 of the Home Guard have rifles or machine guns. Nearly half of the whole Home Guard are veteran soldiers of the last war. Such a Force is of the highest value and importance. A country where every street and every village bristles with loyal, resolute, armed men is a country against which the kind of tactics which destroyed Dutch resistance—tactics of parachutists or air-borne troops in carriers or gliders, Fifth Column activities—if there were any over here, and I am increasingly sceptical—would prove wholly ineffective. A country so defended would not be liable to be overthrown by such tactics. Therefore I agree with those who think that the invasion danger has for the time being diminished. But do not let us make the mistake of assuming that it has passed away, or that it may not occur in more acute form or in some other form.

What is it that has turned invasion into an invasion scare? It is the maintenance in Britain of strong forces and unremitting vigilance by sea, air and land. A mighty army crouches across the Channel and the North Sea, and substantial masses of shipping are gathered in all the harbours of the Western seaboard of Europe, from the North Cape to the Gironde River. We must not let our "shallow-clevers" lead us into thinking that this is all pretence, a manoeuvre to tie us down here and prevent us redisposing our Forces. The vital realities of their duties must be borne in on the whole of our Home Forces and the whole of our Home Guard during these winter months. There must be no relaxation except for necessary leave, but let me say this, that the plain fact that an invasion, planned on so vast a scale, has not been attempted in spite of the very great need of the enemy to destroy us in our citadel and that all these anxious months, when we stood alone and the whole of the world wondered, have passed safely away—that fact constitutes in itself one of the historic victories of the British Isles and is a monumental milestone on our onward march.

THE ART OF PROWLING

By
COLONEL G. A. WADE, M.C.

AUTHOR OF
"The Defence of Bloodford Village," etc.

ALDERSHOT
GALE & POLDEN LIMITED
Price One Shilling net.
(By post 1/2)

SUMMARY

AIR-BORNE ATTACK—NEW PROBLEMS—NEED FOR PROWLERS.

DEFINITION	"*Stealthily* as for *prey* or *plunder*."
FURTIVENESS	combined with CURIOSITY.
STATIONARY	sentry not much use.
OBJECTS	of *Prowling.*
ADVANTAGE	of prowler over sentry.

HOW SHOULD HE MOVE?
> In the shadow.
> Avoiding sticks, etc.
> Glancing back.
> Selection of background.

CUNNING	Examples.
PICTURE	Good prowler.
CAPTURE	of saboteur.
	Clear " Alarm " signal.
	No relaxation.
	Searching of suspect.
SEARCH	for saboteur's pal.
CHALLENGING	Prowler should *not* be in full view when challenging.
	Do not tempt enemy to shoot.
SUSPECT	should be exposed when challenged.
	Not too far away or he may escape.
	Not too close or he may rush the prowler.
CHALLENGE	should be *aggressive* and *loud*.
	" Mein Gott! "
TOUGH GUY	Work bolt after first challenge.
	Do not relax.
PARACHUTIST	Description—How to shoot.
DOUBLE PATROLS	Night or fog.
REAR	man protects comrade.

PROWLERS	must *work together*.
	Danger of *surprise*.
	Risk of *attacking each other*.

APPROACHING SUSPECT

	Best from *two sides*.
	Fire should not be *masked*.

PENETRATION	.303-inch.
	" Seven men, kill eighth."

USE OF NATURE	Birds, beasts, streams, trees, earth.

EVERY MOVEMENT	followed by *keen eyes and ears*.
	All will tell you a lot.
	Blackbirds.
	Rabbits.

JAYS, MAGPIES, TOMTITS give WARNINGS.

TREES	Crackles.
GROUND	Footprints.
STREAMS	Avoidance—Use.

NO ATTEMPT TO LAY DOWN LAW.

SKETCH OF GENERAL PRINCIPLES.

SHORTEN DUTY	by concentrating on prowling.

THE PROWL, INSTEAD OF DULL DUTY, WILL BECOME
FULL OF INTEREST AND EXCITEMENT.

THE ART OF PROWLING

THE development of air-borne attack has furnished the defence of this country with many new problems, not least of which is the keeping of enormous tracts of land under very close observation.

At any time of the day or night the enemy may descend upon us from the skies either with the idea of attacking us forthwith or of proceeding quietly to some vital part, such as a factory, aerodrome, or railway junction, and there perpetrating some act of sabotage which may do tremendous harm to our war effort or our defences.

In the first case, if they attack in bodies they will be met by fighting patrols, but in the second if they disperse and creep towards their objectives it may be necessary for the defence to cover so much ground and to protect so many places that there are not enough troops to do it by large parties, and the area can only be searched or protected by soldiers patrolling singly or in pairs.

These men may cover quite a large expanse during their tour of duty, and they are commonly called " PROWLERS."

A prowl can be either a *bore* or a fascinating *pastime,* according to the point of view of the prowler.

" Prowl " is a splendid word with which to describe moving patrol duties by a soldier. The dictionary definition is: " *To wander stealthily as for prey or plunder.*"

Yes, if the soldier prowls properly he certainly wanders stealthily and his prey is the *saboteur.*

His motto might well be " *Furtiveness* combined with *Curiosity.*"

Good prowling does not consist of just walking round —it is an *art* in itself.

If you want to make your spell of duty pass quickly, concentrate on prowling properly; if you do so, two or three hours will seem like ten minutes.

From the standpoint of preventing sabotage the stationary sentry is not much use. You see, the enemy knows exactly where he is and what he can see. Consequently, the sentry protects only a very small area and his chance of ever catching a saboteur is remote.

The objects of prowling are: —

    (1) To enable one or two men to afford protection over a considerable area.

    (2) To give soldiers on guard duty an opportunity of surprising evilly disposed people.

    (3) To cause would-be saboteurs to have a feeling of uncertainty as to the position of the guards.

Do not forget—the object of the prowler should not be only to prevent sabotage but to *capture* the saboteur.

The great advantage of the prowler over the sentry is that he can move about and you can tell if he is a good prowler or a bad one by the *way* he moves about; in fact, if a prowler can move properly he has mastered 90 per cent. of the great art.

How should he move?

QUIETLY—STEALTHILY—AND WITH *CUNNING!*

It is extraordinary how reluctant the British soldier is to show *cunning*. During the last war thousands of good men lost their lives simply because they scorned to be cunning. Cunning is not one of our national characteristics, and we have a wholesome tendency to dislike cunning people in private life; consequently, we try to play the game of war as if it had highly developed rules for fair play like cricket and football.

The difference is, of course, that in football the rules bind both sides equally, but in the present war any sly, bloody, dirty trick the Germans can employ to forward their ends they do, and hold the victims in scorn for being fool enough to let them.

It is absolutely certain that the German paratroops and, for that matter, Hitler's agents now at large in this country will be as sly as foxes; consequently, unless you realize this and are prepared to fight fire with fire, your usefulness as a prowler will be limited indeed.

In fact, the *whole object of this lecture* is to induce you to take a pride in being really, truly, definitely CUNNING, CRAFTY and SLY.

Let me give you a few examples of what I mean by cunning.

When returning from a prowl do not come back by the same track as that you took on the outward journey; some evilly disposed totalitarian may have seen you go out and decided to " lay for " you as you return.

If you look round a corner and you see nothing, do not let it rest at that, but wait a minute or so and then look again. You may surprise someone who saw you the first time and thinks you have gone.

Incidentally, always look round a corner from ground level first and be sure your second look round is from a standing-up position. Somebody may have seen you and be taking aim in readiness for the reappearance of your head.

If it appears in a different place the enemy has to realign his weapon and you can see the movement in time to jerk your head back.

Occasionally cover your own track by taking a quick, *quiet* sweep to the right or left, doubling back and coming again over the track you have just passed. Some time you may find yourself just behind someone with a dagger who thinks he is still behind *you*!

In this case, you know what to do! But don't stick it up his backside because he will bellow like a bull and your bayonet may stick. A quick, hard thrust at the small of his back will get his kidneys and he will flop without warning the whole neighbourhood.

13

Put one or two pebbles in your pocket when prowling at night. You may find them useful if you wish to distract someone's attention while you get within reach. Just toss the pebble over his head so that it drops somewhere behind him; give him a second to turn that way and then pounce.

That is what I mean by using cunning. You will be able to think out lots of other instances if you will keep your eyes open for the opportunities.

Now let us picture a prowler doing his job properly.

If you look very carefully you will see him in the shadow of that bush. He was not there a minute ago, and where he came from I don't know; he just sort of appeared quietly from nowhere, and he is peering attentively down the side of the building, looking particularly at each patch of bushes and shadow.

Every now and then he glances behind him. Now he moves on, keeping in the shadows so that his khaki blends with the bushes, carefully avoiding any leaves or sticks which would crackle under his feet.

How quickly he crosses that open patch where he can be seen so well, and how he lingers where he cannot be seen!

Do you notice how frequently he looks backward?

What a long time he is in those bushes! Well, I'm bothered! He has just popped up again over there. He must have crept along that ditch.

By Jove, look! There's a suspicious-looking man creeping under those bushes towards the building, and the prowler has not seen him!

In another minute the prowler will have gone round the end of the building, and the sneaking man will get across the open space to the door.

The prowler has a last look backwards and vanishes round the end of the building. That tough-looking guy has been waiting for this, and now he leaves his cover and steps quickly across the open to the vulnerable point.

What a pity the prowler didn't spot him!

But, look! What's that peeping round the end of the building? It's the prowler!

Yet he doesn't challenge the man: he's waiting till he is right out in the open and can't get away.

Now he pounces out! What a bellow of a challenge! Did you see that chap jump? He'd have bolted if the bushes were a bit nearer. Did you notice his knees knock when the prowler rattled his bolt?

How plainly the prowler blew his long and short "Alarm" signals! No mistaking those.

Here comes the guard. By Jove, the prowler does not relax much! It will be heaven help that rough chap if he makes a break!

Look! The Sergeant has found a pistol in the man's pocket and they are marching him to the guard room.

Where is the prowler going to?

Oh, he's dashing off to search round to see if the saboteur had a pal with him!

Now a word about CHALLENGING.

When you are going to challenge a suspected person, remember that there is a right and a wrong way of doing this.

To begin with, do not, if you can help it, challenge when you are in full view and the suspect is not plainly visible. If you are silhouetted plainly against your background and the saboteur is armed, you are tempting him to shoot, whereas the most desperate man will hesitate to resist if he cannot see *you* very well, and knows that *he* is a plain target.

Do not challenge while he is still so far away as to easily escape by jumping into a bush or shadow.

Wait until he is reasonably close, but not near enough to jump on you, and then, suddenly, in a loud, determined voice, with an aggressive attitude and your bayonet thrust forward as if you mean business, challenge *violently* so as to make the suspect say " Mein Gott! This is a *tough guy* got me! "

What is more, *be a tough guy* and make up your mind that if he does not stop after your second " Halt or I fire! " you will stop him with one through the shin.

Don't forget to work your bolt immediately after your first " Halt or I fire! " The rattle of the cartridge going into the breech will help the suspect to stand to attention.

Having got your man, do not relax your vigilance for one moment till either you are satisfied of the man's good faith or the guard has taken him over.

That is how you challenge a SUSPECTED PERSON, that is, someone who *may* be hostile, but also may *not*.

But there is another gentleman you may see who does not come under the category of " suspected person " at all.

You may in your prowling come across a man in a grey suit, wearing a funny sort of tin hat with hardly any rim on, with rubber boots half-way up his calves and a zip fastener down his front. He will probably be carrying an overgrown sort of pistol pointing in your direction and be walking towards you in a purposeful manner.

Do not, in these circumstances, come from under your bit of cover and say " Advance, friend, and be recognized," because this is a traveller in Hitler's goods —Bad Faith, Blood Lust and Sudden Death.

There is only one language he understands, so talk to him in that.

Low down in the chest is the place to aim: keep as still as a mouse till he is so close that you cannot possibly miss and then squeeze the trigger.

As soon as you have done that you can, if it will ease your conscience at all, shout, " Halt or I fire! " This will be quite consistent with Germany's treatment of the smaller nations.

After you have shot the first paratroop do not move, keep very still and wait for the next one. He will *not* come the same way, but will try to get behind you, so look out!

The idea of a double patrol at night or in foggy weather is that the prowler in front, having his safety against attack guaranteed by the prowler behind, can devote all his attention to the job in hand, namely, the spotting of saboteurs.

The rear man can, of course, do a certain amount of spotting likewise, but his primary job is to protect his comrade.

Under conditions of fair visibility the distance the rear prowler lags behind can be more than in dense darkness or fog, but touch must never be lost.

Frequently I see double prowlers who are really not double prowlers at all, but simply two single prowlers working over the same ground. This is quite wrong, as both are liable to treacherous attack. In addition to the uncertainty which must prevail in their minds if they hear sounds and are not sure if it is the other prowler or an enemy, there is the risk of attacking each other.

In connection with night prowling it is surprising how much men's night sight and hearing improve with practice.

Under conditions of modern civilization men have little need to use their eyes in the dark, and consequently it takes some time to accustom them to move quickly and noiselessly in darkness.

It is very interesting to make tests of men's night sight by seeing how many given objects each can see from the same spot.

If two men go out as double prowlers one should be selected for his good night sight and the other for his keen hearing. This makes an ideal combination.

When two prowlers are working properly together it will frequently be possible to approach a suspect from two sides and thus make doubly sure of his capture.

A point to be carefully noted when a man has been challenged and one prowler approaches him while the other covers him, is that the approaching prowler should never mask the fire of the other one.

Incidentally, he should frisk the man for firearms from the side and not get so that the suspect is between him and the other prowler. A .303-inch bullet will go through seven men and kill the eighth!

When prowling make full use of Nature—the BIRDS, the BEASTS, the STREAMS, the TREES, and even the EARTH itself are all on your side if you will let them help.

Do not forget that *your* eyes and *your* ears are not by any means the only ones on your beat. Your every movement is followed by ears and eyes far keener than yours, and, what is more, the movements of any other human intruder are watched very closely; consequently, the birds, the rabbits, the cats, and other animals will tell you quite a lot if you will understand their language.

21

A blackbird's cry of alarm means something to a good prowler and he will not rest till he has discovered its cause.

If a rabbit is quietly grazing and the prowler sees him stop feeding, sit up, raise his big ears, sniff the air and then lollop off, something has disturbed him! It may be a stoat, or a fox, or a cat, but it *may* be a GERMAN.

Jays, magpies, jackdaws, even tomtits, have their own way of reacting to human presence, and they may unwittingly warn a prowler so that he is able to cover himself with glory by saving a vulnerable point.

Trees differ a lot. Some drop leaves and twigs which dry and crackle. These the prowler should note and keep from under, but in the darkness a saboteur may creep beneath it, and the prowler, hearing the rustle and cracking, knows exactly which tree the saboteur is under, and makes his plans accordingly.

Even the ground will help the prowler if he will read the signs. During the last war a swept path was kept down the length of the Suez Canal, and every morning it was examined for footprints which would show that a saboteur had put a mine in the Canal.

In parts of some prowls there is soft clay or sand which can be smoothed over so that footprints will be immediately seen.

If on your prowl there is a stream which babbles noisily along, do not, if you can help it, get too close to it, because you cannot hear much if you do. But remember, if you are stalking a suspect and can let him get close to the stream you can advance quickly upon him with little risk of being heard.

All vulnerable points are different and so are all prowls. Consequently, I have endeavoured not so much to lay down the law as to sketch out the general principles which govern the tactics of the prowler.

It is for you to apply them to your own cases according to circumstances.

Let me in conclusion repeat what I said to begin with. You will find it very true:—

" If you want to make your spell of duty pass quickly, concentrate on prowling properly; if you do so, two or three hours will seem like ten minutes."

THE GOOD PROWLERS MOTTO

RENARDUM SANGUINEA SUNT SED
MEUM TWISTUM NON POSSOMUS
· · · · EST · · · · ·

THIS IS LATIN (WE HOPE)
AND THE TRANSLATION IS —

"THEY MAY BE BLOODY FOXY
BUT THEY CANNOT DIDDLE ME"

NOTES

GALE & POLDEN LTD
PRINTERS · ALDERSHOT

P 9437

A NEW SERIES OF TRAINING BOOKS
By COLONEL G. A. WADE, M.C.
(Author of " The Defence of Bloodford Village ")

s. d.

Fire Control. Illustrated with Landscape Targets in colour   1 6

By Post   1 8

CONTENTS.—Effect on Enemy—Effect on our own Men—Ammunition Supply—Talk about Rifles—Rifle Fire, properly controlled, more deadly than M.Gs.—How Rifles should be Used—Opening and Stopping Fire—Quick Concentration or Distribution—Targets against which Machine-guns Ineffective—Selectivity of Rifle Fire—Avoidance of Casualties—The Key Man in Fire Control—Choice of suitable Fire Positions—Alternative Positions—Selection of Targets—Section should engage Target nearest its Front—The D R I N K Sequence—Four Kinds of Fire Orders—Kinds of Fire—Indication and Recognition—Number of Rounds—Fire Control Competitions—Observations.

The Defence of Towns. Illustrated   ...   (By Post, 1/8)   1 6

CONTENTS.—Four Essential Points—Suitable Training—Tactical Training—House-to-House Fighting—Every House is a Passage—Right Dispositions—All-round Defence—The Keep—The Men and the Weapons—Communications—Mobility—Obstacles—Reserves—Reliefs—Fire Control; Traps; Surprise.

Defence of Houses.   (By Post, 1/8)   1 6

CONTENTS.—Choice of House to Defend—Mutual Support—All-round Defence—Loopholes—Shoring up—The Roof—Entrances—Sanitary Arrangements—Outside—Dominating Positions - Dead Ground—Approaches—Fire—The Men—Automatic Weapons—Bombs and Mines—Snipers—Liaison—Correct Tactics.

Defence of Villages and Small Towns. Illustrated with plates and diagrams in colour   ...   (By Post, 1/8)   1 6

CONTENTS.—Strategic Importance of Villages—What Kind of Attack?—Oppose Fore with Force—Which Parts Vital to Defend?—Need for Reserve—Siting the Keeps—Description of Keeps—Road Blocks—The Fighting Patrols—Men and Weapons—Rounding off the Defence Scheme—Liaison—Block Landing Grounds—Barbed Wire—Communications—Tank Traps—Water in Defence—Shot-guns—Training—Chronological Defence in Depth.

Road Blocks. Illustrated with plates and diagrams. (By Post 1/8)   1 6

CONTENTS.—Importance of Road Blocks—Site your Road Blocks for Defence—Good Sites for Road Blocks—Active Defence of Road Blocks—Specimen Defence Action—Road Blocks in Depth—Mistakes in siting Road Blocks—Halting Traffic at a Distance—Trees—Camouflage—Bluff—Traps—Routine—Orders to Road Block Guard Commanders—Standing Orders for Guards on Road Blocks.

House-to-House Fighting. Illustrated in colour. (By Post 1/8)   1 6

CONTENTS.—Objectives — Surprise — Covering Fire — Observation — Attack from Roofs—Attack through Cocklofts—Attack through Walls—Attacking Houses—Reserves—Smoke—Crossing Streets—Tackling Barricades—Defence of Houses—Cellars—Booby Traps—Street Fighting Competitions—Tanks in Towns.

Factory Defence. Illustrated with diagrams in colours. (By Post 1/8)   1 6

CONTENTS.—Size, Shape, Lay-out—Average Factory can certainly Defend Itself—Countering the Saboteur—Principles to be Observed by Watchmen—Defence against Attack in Force—Split Factory into Vital and Non-Vital Parts—All-round Defence—Strengthening and Provisioning; Fire-fighting Equipment—Alternative Positions—Careful Study of Plan—Aggressive Defence—Kostinoff Brickworks—Final Hints.

The Fighting Patrol. Illustrated in colour.   (By Post, 1/8)   1 6

CONTENTS.—Home Guard Defence—Types of Patrol: Standing Patrol; Reconnoitring Patrol; Fighting Patrol—Objects of Fighting Patrol—Definite Task—Strength—Equipment—Formation—Movement—Unexpected Action—Communications: Field Signals—General Observations.

Fighting Patrol Training. Illustrated in colour   (By Post 1/8)   1 6

CONTENTS.—Training—Six Characteristics—Determination to Attack—Skill in handling Weapons—Ability to move properly—Instinctive Reaction to Attack—Synchronization—Confidence—Street Fighting—How to clear Houses—Fighting Patrol Competitions—Example of Fighting Patrol Exercise—Observations on another Exercise—A Well-planned Fighting Patrol Action—Two Final Hints.

Fighting Patrol Tactics. Illustrated in colour   (By Post 1/8)   1 6

CONTENTS.—Points before Starting—Parachutists—The Attack—The Defence—Night Patrols—Object of Fighting Patrol—Nature on our Side—Trees—Earth—Lie of Land: What to look for—Observation; Deduction; Action—Indoor Training.

Obtainable from all booksellers or direct from the publishers

GALE & POLDEN LTD. ALDERSHOT
also on sale at their showrooms

LONDON: Ideal House, Argyll St., Oxford Circus, W.1
PORTSMOUTH: Nelson House, Edinburgh Road

JUST PUBLISHED

Sir George Wade and the
Gale & Polden Training Series

Philip Abbott

In summer 1940 Britain faced the imminent threat of invasion. Following the fall of France and the evacuation from Dunkirk, British men who were not in military service were encouraged by Anthony Eden, Secretary of State for War, to enrol in the Local Defence Volunteers. 250,000 signed up in the first seven days, only to face a lack of weapons and training manuals. Emergency orders for rifles were placed with Canada, but in the meantime the War Office issued instructions on how to make Molotov cocktails, and local units improvised weapons from whatever was at hand. Although the RAF's victory over the Luftwaffe ensured that the immediate threat of invasion receded, the need for practical training persisted.

In October 1940 Lieutenant Colonel George Wade was approached to write a tactical guide for the new recruits. Wade was a First World War veteran who had joined the army in August 1914 and became an officer in the South Staffordshire Regiment. Later seconded to the Machine Gun Corps, he was awarded the Military Cross and Bar for gallantry at the battle of Gommecourt (1916) and during the breaching of the Hindenberg Line (1918). Wade was recalled to active service at the beginning of the Second World War and placed in command of troops protecting vulnerable points, such as factories and aerodromes, from sabotage. His innovative training techniques would prove a great success in this new commission.

Wade already had examples to draw upon, most notably *The Defence of Duffers Drift* – a short book on minor tactics written in 1904 by Captain E. D. Swinton as a result of his experiences during the Boer War. The book followed the experiences of

'Lieutenant Backsight Forethought', ordered to defend a river crossing from a superior force. Wade explained its value in a letter to a friend:

> D. Drift was a classic, read by all young officers & it was about a subaltern in S. Africa (1900) who was sent to prevent any Boers passing a drift (ford). He went to sleep and dreamt how the Boers go past his defences owing to bad defence scheme. He corrected what was wrong & next night had another dream and the blighters got through again. Each day he corrected his mistakes & each night he had another dream showing the weaknesses. Consequently when the Bs (for Boers, not what you thought!) attacked he repelled them & got the D.S.O.

Wade decided to adopt the same approach. After consulting the official training manuals on village and street fighting he composed *The Defence of Bloodford Village*, in which he described how Geoffrey (Skipper) Gee and the Home Guard held up the German advance and thus contributed to the defeat of the invasion. Wade began by describing the geographical features of the village and the initial dispositions of the defenders to illustrate two of his twenty-eight learning outcomes: the need to cultivate a tactical eye for the ground, and to emphasise the advantage of local knowledge. He then described six scenarios and their outcomes (dreams), each in greater detail, to illustrate the tactical principles necessary to conduct a successful defence of the position.

The Defence of Bloodford Village was issued in November 1940. Around the same time, Wade published a short satirical article entitled "What Happened to Fritz" in *The Vulnerable Point: Magazine of 1/9th Battalion (HD) The Sth. Staffords Regt*, which described the fate of Fritz Gestaponberg during the German invasion of 1940. Fritz was part of a tank unit, which was intended to break through the defending British troops spreading alarm and consternation in the rear. However, the tank soon became isolated and was stalked by members of the Home Guard who opened fire every time it stopped moving. The tank also encountered determined opposition from the public: a "buxom, blonde and beautiful" girl who responded to Fritz's advances by throwing a Molotov cocktail at the tank; an old women who threw a flat iron at Fritz, hitting him in the mouth and shattering his teeth; an old man who inserted a pick-head between the driving sprocket and the track, bringing the tank to a halt; children, who set fire to a barn in which the tank was sheltering from hostile aircraft; and the four labourers who pushed a farm roller down a hill, throwing the tank sideways and almost turning it over. Wade's core theme – that it was the duty of every man, woman and child to resist the invasion – is reminiscent of the Soviet defence of the motherland against the Germans. However, it was couched in typical British humour. At one stage, Fritz is caught short and dashes behind a hedge: "Hardly had he vanished from view when there were two reports from a shotgun and Fritz dashed back trying to run and pull up his trousers at the same time".

Wade, now in command of the important Birkenhead Sector of the Mersey Garrison, was encouraged to write a series of pamphlets by Gale & Polden of Aldershot, a well-established publisher of books on military administration and training. The series was intended to supplement the official War Office publications by offering practical advice to the Home Guard. The full series comprised *House to House Fighting*, *The Art of Prowling*, *The Fighting Patrol*, *Fighting Patrol Training*, *Fighting Patrol Tactics*, *Defence of Villages and Small Towns*, *Road Blocks*, *Factory Defence*, *Defence of Towns*, *Fire Control*, *Defence of Houses* and Intelligence and Liaison. A list of in-press pamphlets printed on the inside front cover of *Fighting Patrol Training* included *Anti-Tank Traps*, *Camouflage*, *Cyclist Patrols* and *Field Engineering* but these were never published.

The individual pamphlets were intended to contribute to a general scheme of defence, which Wade outlined in *The Fighting Patrol*. The first part of the scheme consisted of towns and villages, which should be "defended by all-round defensive posts situated at tactical points", near the centre of which would be a "keep" or strong point capable of being held against a considerable force. Within the defensive posts and the "keep" would be mobile detachments ready to "sally forth and smite any enemy located within hitting distance". The pamphlets on *Defence of Villages and Small Towns* and *Defence of Towns* form the key publications in the first sub-series, whilst the others (as their titles suggest) provide more detailed information on *House-to-House Fighting*, *Defence of Houses*, *Factory Defence*, *Fire Control*, *Road Blocks*, and *Intelligence and Liaison*. The second part of the scheme consists of fighting patrols, which would "systematically and regularly cover the country round their defensive posts" to prevent bodies of enemy troops (particularly parachutists) from either surprising the main defences or sending forward reconnaissance patrols, and to constantly harass and hinder his progress. This sub-series comprises the three pamphlets on *The Fighting Patrols*, *Fighting Patrol Training* and *Fighting Patrol Tactics* (intended to be read in conjunction with one another), and the supplementary pamphlet on *The Art of Prowling*.

Wade began each pamphlet with a brief introduction, in which he set out a particular strategic situation or tactical problem. He examined either the enemy's likely mode of attack, or the tactical development of tanks, paratroopers and saboteurs, and how these might be defied. All too aware that the use of airborne troops created numerous new problems for the defence of the country, he wrote of the critical need for effective fighting patrols – especially if paratroopers had dispersed widely over the countryside. Such large areas of ground, Wade believed, could only be searched or protected by soldiers patrolling singly or in pairs.

In the three key pamphlets of the second sub-series Wade examined the different types of fighting patrol, their purpose, organisation and operation (both by day and night), much of which would fall to platoon, section and squad leaders. He also emphasised the importance of understanding the countryside: knowing the places where the enemy might be lying, noting the warnings of a human presence offered by moving birds or animals, and the need to make a covered approach. He returned to the subject of the use of nature in more detail in *The Art of Prowling*.

Wade included detailed examples to illuminate the tactical problems, such as the fight at The Mairie (*Defence of Houses*) and the attack on the Kostinoff Brickworks (*Factory Defence*), all of which were supported by clearly-drawn plans and diagrams. In the pamphlets on *House-to-House Fighting* and the *Defence of Houses* he also used line drawings to illustrate the progress of a fighting patrol, the role of scouts, street fighting and house clearance. By contrast, the illustrations in *The Art of Prowling* are much more in the form of rough sketches. Wade drew widely on his knowledge of historical events: *Fire Control* featured examples from the Battles of Bunker Hill (1775) and Waterloo (1815) in an attempt to encourage the ordinary solder to look after his weapons and develop his skills of marksmanship.

Wade intended that the pamphlets should be used to facilitate training, rather than simply read or used as the basis of lectures. Some contain exercises, such as the well-planned patrol on the road to Caldos (*Fighting Patrol Training*), or treasure hunts and spy chases that encouraged map reading and field sketching (*Intelligence and Liaison*). Others included suggestions for competitions that were carefully planned to test different skills and develop teamwork. In a street-fighting competition the teams were ordered to destroy enemy-occupied houses, put homes into a state of defence, and block a road against the enemy's advance (*House-to-House Fighting*). In *Fighting Patrol Training* they take

35

part in shooting, dummy grenade throwing and a fighting patrol action. Finally, *Fire Control* featured a competition to test both the teams' shooting skills as well as the section leader's ability to select positions, use cover and engage targets.

Wade usually concluded the main text of his pamphlets with a last few hints followed by words of inspiration. In some he tried to infect his readers with his own enthusiasm, encouraging them to "make your practice into a great game, for that is what house-to-house fighting really is" (*House-to-House Fighting*). In others he used almost Churchillian rhetoric, reminding them that "if every industrial plant in the path of the invader puts up a stubborn defence the effect upon the whole campaign will be immense, and very likely decisive" (*Factory Defence*). Perhaps the most memorable is found in *The Art of Prowling*, where The Good Prowler's badge bears the Latin motto, "They may be bloody foxy but they cannot diddle me".

The Gale & Polden Training Series was evidently very successful. Wade was subsequently asked to write the official training manual on minor tactics for the Home Guard, which was issued in four parts as *Battlecraft and Battle Drill for the Home Guard (Home Guard Instruction No. 51)*. He observed in the foreword that there was nothing very new about battlecraft or battle drill, and that the Home Guard had picked up many versions of both from the field army. However, although Wade urged the Home Guard to master the drills, his emphasis as a practical man endured: "Do not become a slave to battle drill at the expense of battlecraft".

Also from Royal Armouries Publishing

House to House Fighting

THE GALE & POLDEN
TRAINING SERIES

HOUSE TO HOUSE
FIGHTING
by COL. G.A.WADE, M.C. *Author of "The Defence of Bloodford Village" etc.*

Price 1/6 net. by post 1/8

Do you know that house-to-house fighting is the finest sport on earth?

Do you know that is it just the sort of close-quarter scrapping we British excel in?

Do you know that once you get going you will *love* it?

Do you want to come with me down our street and play hell with some bloody Huns?

You do?

Right, we'll carry on!

·DEFENCE·
OF HOUSES
by COL.G.A.WADE,M.C.
Author of "The Defence of Bloodford Village" etc.

THE GALE & POLDEN
TRAINING SERIES

Price 1/6 net. by post 1/8

When the enemy invade us the most stubborn fighting will be in the built-up areas where their tanks will not be able to help them much.

Houses are found in infinite variety. Some are suited for defence, others are absolute death-traps.

Think: is it strong? Has it a cellar? Are its surrounding suitable? Is it capable of all-round defence?

Let me impress upon you once again: let your defence be active; go out and hit the enemy first; keep hitting him as he draws near to your defended house; and have your defences so good and so cunning, both inside and outside, that when he begins to attack it you can heave a sigh of relief and say, 'And now he's going to ask for it, and he *will* get it!'

The Fighting Patrol

Never take a man with a cough on patrol.

Beats on the ground with the palm or the fist will travel a long way, and if done artistically may suggest rabbits to a listening enemy. A birdlike whistle is passable but not quite so good, and of course, the romantic thing is the hoot of an owl.

Whispering can carry a long way at night and may give the whole show away.

Places where there are crackly twigs should be avoided and care should be taken not to alarm the birds and beasts of the countryside any more than can be helped. Jays and magpies can be a terrible nuisance and will, if disturbed, follow a patrol for hundreds of yards, chattering like a W.V.S. sewing party and alarming the whole countryside.